GENERATION Y IN BUSINESS

Tips for building strong relationships between generations

Written by Pierre Latour
Translated by Emma Lunt

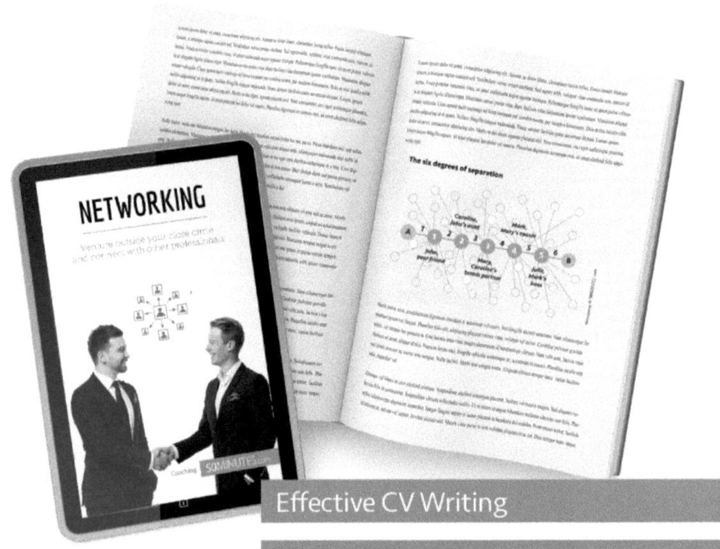
50MINUTES.com

PROPEL
YOUR BUSINESS FORWARD!

NETWORKING
Venture outside your close circle
and connect with other professionals

Coaching 50MINUTES.com

The six degrees of separation

Effective CV Writing

Resolving Office Conflict

Boost Your Concentration

Find Your Work-Life Balance

www.50minutes.com

GENERATION Y IN BUSINESS: WHAT'S CHANGED?   1

GENERATION Y IN THE WORKING WORLD: THE BASICS 3

The different generations

An evolution of professional behaviour

What are the consequences for organisations?

Intergenerational relations in business

Productivity and harmony within the organisation

In summary

TOP TIPS   21

FAQS   25

What are the characteristics of Generation Y?

What can I do right now to improve intergenerational relationships in my organisation?

How should I react if an intergenerational conflict breaks out in the middle of a meeting?

Should I manage generations differently?

Does an organisation transform when it comes into contact with Generation Y?

OVER TO YOU   27

Exercise 1 – Understand the situation

Exercise 2 – Facing conflict

FURTHER READING   30

GENERATION Y IN BUSINESS: WHAT'S CHANGED?

- **Issue:** what changes do Generation Y bring to organisations and professional relationships? How can we resolve this intergenerational issue?
- **Uses:** defining the challenges and optimising intergenerational relationships so as to establish a calm and productive working environment.
- **Professional context:** professional relationships, team management, intergenerational management.
- **FAQs:**
  - What are the characteristics of Generation Y?
  - What can I do right now to improve intergenerational relationships in my organisation?
  - How should I react if an intergenerational conflict breaks out in the middle of a meeting?
  - Should I manage generations differently?
  - Does an organisation transform when it comes into contact with Generation Y?

For several years, Generation Y has been increasingly present within organisations, reviving the issue of intergenerational conflict, which returns every 25 years or so with the arrival of a new generation. This cyclic demographic phenomenon is unfortunately never problem-free and, as no company can permanently deal with conflictual human relationships, it is important to take the specifics of each group into account in order to establish a balance. We can now look at the cultural gaps between different generations, which sometimes stop them from working together in harmony. They do not always have the same moral vision, the same understanding of hierarchy or even the same results-focused culture. Indeed, these generations have received different educations depending on the era in which they were born. Their social context and life journeys are different, as the world has evolved over the decades. Business does not escape these issues, as working relationships are also affected.

Currently, reactivity and flexibility are essential qualities for an organisation. Their direct competitors are no longer only situated within their area, city or country, but across the entire world. They must permanently adapt by producing better, cheaper products. In this environment where competitivity prevails, 25-year-olds work in close collaboration with colleagues who are 30 years older. This type of situation does not occur without causing interpersonal problems that must be dealt with constructively. Communication can sometimes prove to be very complicated between generations, as their experiences and cultural references are sometimes diametrically opposed.

In 50 minutes, you can learn from the reflections and practical advice provided in this little guide. It is aimed at all those who are progressing in business: the manager and the HR director, but also employees of all generations. We are taking up the challenge of guiding in this meaningful yet difficult task, namely and reducing intergenerational divides.

GENERATION Y IN THE WORKING WORLD: THE BASICS

THE DIFFERENT GENERATIONS

Currently, several generations work together in organisations: baby-boomers (born 1945-1960), Generation X (born 1960-1980) and those that followed, logically named Generation Y or the 'Digital Natives' (born 1980-2000). Generation Z is also slowly beginning to appear in working life. Making these four generations work together is a real challenge that organisations must be able to resolve.

Baby-boomers 1945-1960	Generation X 1960-1980	Generation Y 1980-2000	Generation Z From 2000

Generation Y or 'Generation Internet'

We can start by better understanding Generation Y. Learning to decode them in order to get to know them better, without reading too much into their habits or attitudes, is the winning strategy.

On a tram, a young girl checks her emails on her tablet while listening to music. As simple as it may be, this image of a contemporary young person says a lot. Indeed, this generation symbolises a new approach to ICT (information and communication technologies) with a more playful use of this culture, increasingly likened to fun. The variety of media supports and interconnectivity of devices have further accentuated this trend: mobile phones take photographs and receive emails, and computers download music and images immediately. This technical evolution has amplified the demand for 'everything, right now', characterised by the culture of 'zapping' (which refers to a 'zapper', or television remote control that allows you to change the television channel from a distance). Furthermore, the term 'surfer' on the internet reveals the superficiality of intent and the immediacy of desire.

Generation Y is the generation that has taken ownership of mobile objects that enable them to work by being permanently connected, thus giving rise to a new approach to time. Work, entertainment, family life and daily tasks are more interlinked than ever before. The preceding generations were not, however, strangers to the changes that have arisen over the years. While many employees from the previous generation have managed to adapt to ICT in their companies, many others have fallen significantly behind in mastering these new electronic processes. The intergenerational divide is a reality that generates frustration and misunderstanding: it is at the root of many conflicts and dysfunctions within teams in companies. This gap appeared without warning through the replacement of middle managers who, in their daily lives, are used to the tools that are increasingly used at work (smartphones or tablets that have the same kind of language as computers).

AN EVOLUTION OF PROFESSIONAL BEHAVIOUR

Beyond their affinity for computing, Generation Y has a different relationship with work and organisation:

- **Questioning of authority.** As well as the consequences of the current technological revolution on behaviour, those born after the social upheaval of the 1960s have a different relationship with authority and work than previous generations. Human relationships within the organisation have evolved, although this is still mainly organised hierarchically. Generation Y brings together the children of those who have learnt to question the authority of adults and the hierarchy. As a consequence, some behaviours, such as external signs of respect ('politeness'), have seen a shift, although they have fortunately not disappeared completely.
- **Work-life balance.** For this generation, work does not hold the same place that it did for their parents. Family life, friendships and leisure are as fundamental for them as their job. Personal life sometimes even comes before working life. Many young people take a break in their career or a gap year, when their working life is only just beginning. In their search for coherence and meaning, they do not see work as an end in itself, but rather as one instrument among many to thrive.
- **The importance of the working environment.** The atmosphere, the building, smoking areas and even the enjoyment of their commute have become priorities for this generation.

- **A less unionised and politicised generation.** Although this generation is not disinterested in work nor its political environment, it sometimes gives this impression to older generations. Members of Generation Y do not feel very concerned and also have little representation at this level.
- **A desire for recognition.** Despite there being more than 7 billion inhabitants on earth in 2015 compared to 5 billion in 1995, these young people want to stand out from the crowd and be individually recognised.
- **A connected generation.** Media, the internet and social networks are totally integrated in their culture and their way of communicating. This also impacts the many organisations that have adapted themselves to the practices of e-commerce and social networking. Information must spread quickly and constantly.

WHAT ARE THE CONSEQUENCES FOR ORGANISATIONS?

A country's companies reflect all the diversity of human activity. It is therefore dangerous to draw set rules from a phenomenon that influences entities as diverse as multinationals or small artisanal companies. We can nevertheless try to evaluate the consequences that the arrival of Generation Y brings within organisations.

BUSINESS: A HUMAN ADVENTURE

At this stage in our reflection, it is undoubtedly useful to remind ourselves what exactly what a business is. It is a group of individuals who are equipped with material and immaterial, human and financial means, and who come together in order to produce goods and services through strategies and action plans. This group of people is organised in teams that work to ensure longevity as well as profitability. This collective acts within a specific sociocultural framework to which they adapt.

The progressive adaptation towards ICT

The major change brought about by Generation Y, but also by the circumstances of ICT development, is a new relationship to media and communication. Indeed, companies all have the internet now and do their work taking into account the significance of social media. Generation Y has an uninhibited approach to ICT and to technology in general. This phenomenon has been a powerful factor in increasing productivity and creativity; jobs change and employees adapt.

FROM DRIVER TO MANAGER

Let's use the job of a delivery driver as an example. Barely 20 years ago, this involved waiting for a load then going to a given place where responsibility for the merchandise was handed to another team.

Nowadays, the same employee has to be personally responsible for their goods, through sophisticated tools. They can check the state of their stock anytime from their cabin and a barcode system used during un-loading instantly tells the company of the movement of supplies, products, etc. In the space of a few years, the nature of their job has evolved: the deliverer has also become the manager of stock.

Organisations connected to ICT and, more generally, to research and innovation are henceforth the most popular with Generation Y. Facebook, Google or Apple, for example, are very popular with young job-seekers. Working at these companies is good for their image, and the fact that they appear as 'winners' plays a part in this search for meaning that preoccupies the generation. Unlike their elders, it is no longer simply a question of survival or 'getting by', but adding value, particularly professional value, to their lives. This generation's creativity is the result of the evolution of teaching as regards children and a culture of accessible information for everybody. This benefits organisations who, thanks to their input, are refreshing their image and, above all, adapting their products to new consumers.

An evolution in terms of management

In order to establish a productive dynamic, it therefore becomes necessary to adapt management practices to the characteristics of each of the generations present in the organisation. By responding to everybody's expectations and respecting the identity of each individual, collaboration will be much easier.

For example, for Generation Y who aspire to have more

freedom and flexibility at work, it is useful to be able to adjust working hours and to introduce telecommuting. This latter method, which allows employees to work from home, responds particularly well to this generation's need for autonomy and independence.

Another aspect which must be taken into account is their weak attachment to the organisation. Company loyalty is no longer apparent. Successive economic crises have shown the fragility of employment. We can see this profound, contemporary change in Generation Y: the reality of the working world is such that young employees must often change position and company. They are thus convinced that they will not spend their entire working life in the same place. They no longer imagine their professional journey in a linear way nor even in the same sector or one country. They nevertheless need to feel recognised in their work, to move forward and to innovate. If their position does not satisfy their curiosity and desire to progress, they will undoubtedly leave to look elsewhere.

The recruitment process has also evolved. When practiced by the previous generation on Generation Y candidates, it has proved to be full of pitfalls that are at the root of many recruitment errors. Norms between these generations have changed. Effective recruitment must also be accompanied by a policy aimed at retaining talent through tactics including, but not limited to, material benefits. As Generation Y is looking for meaning, fulfilment and personal satisfaction, development is as important to them as remuneration, although this also plays a part. Setting objectives for young employees to achieve with profit-sharing based on results is undoubtedly more influential than raises based on experience or seniority. This is all the more true given that, in the minds of employees from this generation, the true hierarchy is based on competence and creativity rather than title and years of experience. Large companies which have a human resources department have understood this divide more quickly than others, and have thus managed to take advantage of the specifics of Generation Y more quickly.

INTERGENERATIONAL RELATIONS IN BUSINESS

The secret lies in successfully forming groups of diverse profiles – from all generations – within the various departments. Consequently, you should not consider the management of Generation Y outside of this framework. It makes no sense here to treat a generation in a specific way, when the generation itself is made up of individuals with different personalities, from diverse social backgrounds and with varied skills.

How do the generations see themselves?

This is a delicate question. It is therefore worthwhile to avoid jumping to hasty conclusions. The stereotypes are almost always false and, at best, useless. With this major caveat, any scenario can be envisaged, as organisations are only a reflection of human diversity. Here is how the different generations typically perceive each other in a professional setting:

Older employees see themselves and are seen by Generation Y as:	Generation Y employees see themselves and are seen as:
• Logical • Rational • Structured • Experienced • Loyal • Serious • Not very creative	• Dynamic • Undisciplined • Inexperienced • Flexible • Disorganised • Creative

How should you manage several generations together?

While it is not mission impossible, this type of management can nevertheless lead to different reactions following situations and be a source of conflict. For example, a cancelled project will often be viewed as a failure by older employees and as a useful experience by younger people, or a conflict will be judged according to its impact on the organisation by the older generation and as a personal affair by younger employees.

In his book *Intégrer et manager la generation Y* ['*Integrating and managing Generation Y'*], the expert Julien Pouget explains that the challenge of this intergenerational problem is the transmission of values, habits and customs by the most experienced employees. The goal is to make a connection between their knowledge and that brought by this 'digital' generation to create a synergy rather than accentuating the divisions. The mistake to avoid at all costs is therefore pitting generations against one another, as this situation can create tensions of which, sooner or later, the organisation will bear the consequences.

The managerial strategy consequently involves setting objectives that are adapted to each person and which lead towards a shared goal. Are you ready to take on the challenge?

PRODUCTIVITY AND HARMONY WITHIN THE ORGANISATION

Creating routines

The sociocultural situation is constantly and quickly evolving. The world has entered a new era culturally, while businesses are adapting their relationship with the world. Routines, which are temporal and existential reference points, are very important in this shifting situation: they govern collective life and are essential for the cohesion of a group or company. Their usefulness becomes even more evident when several generations coexist. Routines are obviously different from one organisation to another but they remain useful, as they structure the working day. Limiting routines to chats around the coffee machine reflects poor management which, in the end, influences the motivation of their personnel. Generation Y employees are more individualistic than their elders, which makes the strategy of belonging to the organisation even more important to maintain and reinforce team spirit.

Acting together

The manager of a company may cultivate the motivation of employees by keeping people of the same age together. Over time, this attitude harms social cohesion. Working together is the very essence of the business project and the key to peaceful intergenerational relationships. The ideal is for everybody to find the place that best suits them, where they are the most productive. People with experience, and therefore of a certain age, naturally tend to be placed in positions that require proven expertise. The same logic puts the youngest people in simple positions. These situations cause employees to be surrounded only by people like them and accentuate the generational gap. Avoid restricting only one age category to an activity and promote collaboration between people from different generations. It is in fact shared working that will build bonds and alleviate the suspicion generated by prejudices linked to age.

Recognising and respecting others

Being open to other people is difficult when we feel that our true value is not being recognised and we are not being respected. The key to peaceful relationships between humans is the recognition of the individual as they are, and of their skills. Thus, generations must be considered for what they are: having experienced the war, for example, is a strong marker that should not be hidden. Similarly, young people must not feel guilty for having avoided the trauma of a bloody conflict. Furthermore, recognition and respect within a group forms part of the fundamental needs according to the American psychologist Abraham Maslow (1908-1970).

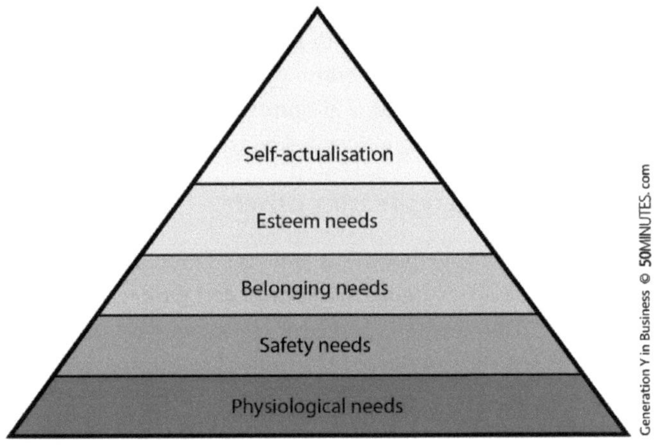

The satisfaction of these needs is the source of personal motivation and development. The skills of each person, whatever their age and position, must therefore be publicly recognised. This means clearly defining the differences and limits to what each person can do and emphasising these. Recognising and respecting the values of the other person improves professional relationships and motivates employees.

Establishing consensual codes of conduct

It is impossible to avoid exchange between colleagues. Incidentally, not wanting to communicate is often the clearest message! Nonverbal communication is very powerful: gestures, looks and attitudes are often more expressive than words. Misunderstandings between generations sometimes come from poor communication or interpretation.

As the codes for 'living in harmony' that improve social relationships have been changed over the years, each generation sees things in a markedly different way. In business, it is necessary to show politeness. As interpersonal codes of politeness are a consensual base for behaviour and values that can be demonstrated with simple words, everybody must keep them in mind, because they promote respect for others and encourage intergenerational harmony.

Uniting the team around external activities

Getting to know each other is one of the best ways to develop friendships or, at the very least, maintain cordial relationships. This being said, it is sometimes difficult to build true connections within companies due to the stress of work and a lack of time or opportunity to speak to one another. Whether through a sporting event among colleagues or just a drink after work, meeting up in a more relaxed situation pacifies relationships and enables us to slightly change our perceptions of certain co-workers.

Buying into the company's myth

Introducing the organisation, in a brochure or on a website, accentuates employees' need to belong. In fact, the company's history is a necessary myth for cohesion. It invites the employee to:

- take an interest in the origins of the organisation, its teachings and its essential values;
- live within a reference framework that reinforces the

company's cultural identity;
* respond to their need to be exemplary.

Each individual must be aware that they are contributing to collective work. This feeling of belonging will ease the intergenerational gap and facilitate human relations at the same time.

Granting intergenerational bonuses

When the need for recognition affects all generations, employees should be congratulated, publicly and across generations as often as possible. The implementation of a skill-based rather than an age-based hierarchy reinforces the feeling of fairness. In no circumstances should rewards encourage presenteeism or age be considered an asset.

Organise joint training

No dynamic organisation can overlook training for its employees. Technological evolution stuns us with its speed. Adapting to a changing environment is essential.

Generation Y is much more comfortable than others in the handling of new digital tools and, more generally, the internet. Digital divides appear between generations. And these are not without consequences! To overcome them, it is a good idea to exchange knowledge through joint training, as young people have the knowledge to pass on to the older generation and vice versa. Indeed, the latter's experience is not obsolete at all. They are keen to communicate their know-how as well as the organisation's habits and customs. The important thing is to create a connection between the firm's fundamental knowledge and that of each generation. Through mutual assistance, each person acquires new skills and relationships become less strained.

Establish a mentoring scheme

Good human resources management promotes constructive intergenerational relationships. Welcoming a new colleague, who is often young, into a department is made much easier if an older employee is made responsible for their training. By being invited to take the apprentice under their wing for a certain amount of time, the experienced employee will naturally create bonds. Furthermore, this type of collaboration within the company immediately proves to be very useful during periods of doubt, potential difficulties or hitches along the way.

Get an intergenerational mediator involved

Conflicts are inevitable within a group. When the manager makes a decision, they leave the wounds open. A mediator, on the other hand, does not decide anything but helps the parties find a solution together, so that future collaboration is possible. To do this, they must be aware of the intergenerational problem.

State the intergenerational problem freely

Consider establishing a space where opinions can be freely expressed. Intergenerational issues can be put forward there without taboo so as to find effective answers. It is important to be able to talk about the problem even within the organisation, as this enables the search for a resolution rather than just hiding the issue. Furthermore, freedom of speech is essential to the wellbeing of employees.

IN SUMMARY

Applying one or several of the tips listed above enables you to improve your working environment and reduce the intergenerational gap. Removing it completely is a utopian dream and goes against the common good. Each individual keeping to themselves a little is also a criterion for wellbeing. These tips cannot be adapted to every organisation but its participants, from all generations, will undoubtedly find inspiration here to progress towards more peaceful relationships.

THINGS TO REMEMBER

- Removing the intergenerational gap is a utopian dream and would go against the common good.
- For the wellbeing of every employee, it is essential that everybody can keep to themselves in their personal space.

Do not forget that in terms of human resource management nothing is ever completely accomplished.

TOP TIPS

- **Bring generations together over a project:** when a new project begins, bring together different generations so as to optimise its chance of success. This means avoiding the project being seen as old and irrelevant if it is led only by older people, or young people's ideas being viewed sceptically by the older generation. If your organisation does not lend itself to the creation of innovative products or inventive methods, form an intergenerational reflection committee on topics concerning the future of the company.
- **Give each person a title that corresponds to their function:** all the positions held throughout the organisation must have a title, or a clear grading, and be understandable and known by all. It is sometimes difficult or tedious to distinguish between all the functions. Force yourself to clarify these points, as eveybody's need for recognition, provided that it is satisfied, is the basis for all group harmony.
- **Remind people of the behavioural rules just as with security and hygiene rules:** as we explained above, behaviour is the first indicator of the divide that exists between generations. Poorly understood attitudes can be a source of frustration and tension. You must therefore avoid any misunderstanding.

- **Plan outings and sporting events for colleagues:** even with limited financial resources, it is possible to create an association or club with an organisation. Made up of men and women from different generations, it could perhaps organise group sports screenings and trips to the cinema/ to see a documentary that is related to the company's flagship product. At the same time, do not hesitate to organise after work drinks where employees can mingle more easily, as they will feel more relaxed.
- **Ensure that the employees know the company's history:** if you do not have an explicative brochure, the website must clearly explain the company's history so as to reinforce the feeling of belonging among employees.

- **Present the organisational structure in an original way from an intergenerational perspective:** beyond the aforementioned differences between Generation Y and their predecessors, there may also be commonalities based around shared values, such as caring about doing work well, kindness or security. While your organisation can emphasise other shared values, they must take care to clearly transmit the organisational structure in a spirit of intergenerational harmony.

- **Promote skill sharing:** while Generation Y have many things to teach their elders, particularly when it comes to ICT, the opposite is also true. Even if these exchanges of knowledge do not have a direct connection to work, they can be beneficial in terms of integration.
- **Form partnerships:** as it is necessarily the older people who take responsibility for teaching the new recruits upon their arrival, why not make the most of this first meeting to form partnerships? Furthermore, if the participants get on well, this type of collaboration can lead to lasting mentorship.
- **Appoint two mediators, of whom one is from Generation Y:** the majority of conflicts stem from a lack of communication and recognition. Rather than resigning yourself to listening to unconstructive remarks, appoint two mediators from different generations to resolve conflicts before they get out of hand.

- **Summarise the development of the intergenerational**

issue in the annual social audit: as the social audit is obligatory, make the most of it to carry out an in-depth analysis of the state of the social situation of the company's employees. Job-seekers from Generation Y will not miss the chance to check the audit of organisations where they hope to be hired. Establishing an active intergenerational policy can prove to be excellent for your organisation's image. But you must let people know!

FAQS

WHAT ARE THE CHARACTERISTICS OF GENERATION Y?

Generation Y brings together individuals from different social and cultural backgrounds. Nonetheless, we can identify some common characteristics, such as:

- familiarity with new information and communication technologies (daily use of the internet and social networks, for example);
- questioning authority;
- impatience due to the culture of 'zapping';
- curiosity and a will to innovate;
- other interests besides work (leisure, family);
- etc.

WHAT CAN I DO RIGHT NOW TO IMPROVE INTERGENERATIONAL RELATIONSHIPS IN MY ORGANISATION?

Follow this advice:

- be aware of the extent of the problem;
- increase intergenerational collaborations in every department;
- organise events to encourage employees from different generations to meet one another outside the office;
- bring generations together around shared projects, to find effective solutions.

HOW SHOULD I REACT IF AN INTERGENERATIONAL CONFLICT BREAKS OUT IN THE MIDDLE OF A MEETING?

Firstly, do not treat it as such, but be well aware of disparities that set these generations against one another. Then designate two mediators, both coming from different generations, to try to resolve the conflict.

SHOULD I MANAGE GENERATIONS DIFFERENTLY?

Absolutely not: this may increase misunderstandings and mistrust, as well as creating a feeling of unfairness. Everybody must be treated in the same way.

DOES AN ORGANISATION TRANSFORM WHEN IT COMES INTO CONTACT WITH GENERATION Y?

Let's be realistic; company dynamics have changed because the psychosocial environment has evolved. Generation Y is only one noticeable element of this evolution, and the working world adapts itself as generations and their behaviours evolve. The people from this generation bring a new relationship with ICT and hierarchy.

OVER TO YOU

EXERCISE 1 – UNDERSTAND THE SITUATION

This short questionnaire will help you to better analyse the current situation in your organisation in terms of intergenerational relationships. By understanding the ins and outs of these relationships, it will be easier for you to find clear areas for improvement.

In your organisation	Yes	No
Do many generations work together?		
Do conflicts occur only between generations?		
Are the generations separated in different departments?		
Can you speak freely about generational differences?		
Do the generations communicate outside work (coffee break, lunch break, etc.)?		
Have events already been organised outside the office for all employees?		
Is generational diversity emphasised?		
Can the generations exchange their knowledge and skills?		
Is each person respected and recognised for who they are and what they have done?		

EXERCISE 2 – FACING CONFLICT

Answer the following questions:

- Have you already faced an intergenerational conflict at work?
- If so, how did you react?
- What solutions were found and adopted?
- Do you think that this conflict could have been resolved differently? If so, how?

We want to hear from you!
Leave a comment on your online library
and share your favourite books on social media!

FURTHER READING

BIBLIOGRAPHY

- Ferry, L. (2015) Jeremy Rifkin, un gourou chez les Bisounours. *Le Figaro*. [Online]. [Accessed 6 August 2015]. Available from: <http://www.lefigaro.fr/vox/economie/2015/07/08/31007-20150708ARTFIG00206-jeremy-rifkin-un-gourou-chez-les-bisounours.php>
- Morley, C. Bia Figueiredo, M., Baudoin, E. and Hrascinec Salierno, A. (2012) *La generation Y dans l'entreprise. Mythes et réalités*. Paris: Pearson.
- Ollivier, D. (2014) Finalités et enjeux du management intergénérationnel. *Le journal du net*. [Online]. [Accessed 6 August 2015]. Available from: <http://www.journal-dunet.com/management/expert/59544/finalites-et-en-jeux-du-management-intergenerationnel.shtml>
- Pouget, J. (2013) *Intégrer et manager la génération Y*. Paris: Vuibert.

ADDITIONAL SOURCES

- Martinson, J. (2016) *Generation Y and the New Work Ethic*. Saskatchewan (Canada): Martrain Corporate and Personal Development.
- Tulgan, B. (2015) *Not Everyone Gets A Trophy: How to Manage the Millennials*. San Francisco: Jossey-Bass.

IMPROVE YOUR GENERAL KNOWLEDGE

IN A BLINK OF AN EYE !

www.50minutes.com